A
MEMORY
for
T · I · N · O

A MEMORY for T·I·N·O

Leo Buscaglia

ILLUSTRATIONS BY

Carol Newsom

Published in the United States of America by:
SLACK, Incorporated
6900 Grove Road
Thorofare, New Jersey 08086
In the United States, distributed to the trade by:
William Morrow and Company, Inc.
105 Madison Avenue
New York, New York 10016

In Canada, distributed to the trade by:
MacMillan of Canada
a Division of Canada Publishing Corporation
164 Commander Boulevard
Agincourt, Ontario
M1S3C7
SLACK, Inc. ISBN: 1-55642-020-X

Library of Congress Cataloging-in-Publication Data
Buscaglia, Leo F.
A memory for Tino / by Leo Buscaglia : illustrated by Carol Newsom.
p.   cm.
Published by SLACK, Inc.
Distributed by Morrow Junior Books.
Summary: A little boy wonders what it is like to have a "memory"
and his new friendship with an elderly neighbor results in a
beautiful one.
ISBN 0-688-07482-0.   ISBN 0-688-07483-9 (lib. bdg.)
[1. Friendship—Fiction.   2. Old age—Fiction.]   I. Newsom, Carol, ill.
II. Title.
PZ7.B957Me   1988
87-28180   [Fic]—dc19
CIP   AC

To my dear friend,
Buddy Zais,
who has enriched the lives
of so many through his giving

Author's Note

This story is true, though the names and certain incidents have been changed. There is a real Tino, and a real Mrs. Sunday. I hope there always will be.

CONTENTS

YOU GIVE BUT LITTLE WHEN YOU GIVE OF
YOUR POSSESSIONS. IT IS WHEN YOU GIVE OF
YOURSELF THAT YOU TRULY GIVE.

—Kahlil Gibran

Have you ever had a memory and wondered how it got there? This is the story of Tino, who gave a gift and got a wonderful memory in return.

CHAPTER ONE

THE MEETING

For Tino, going to and from school was the best part of his day. He always walked to school with his friend Samuel. Each day was a new adventure for them. They would first hunt for stones to throw at clusters of dates hanging from the tall palm trees that lined the street. They would stop just long enough to provoke the Wilsons' dog into barking and jumping wildly against the chain-link fence that enclosed him. But what brought them the greatest pleasure was snooping around the yard of Mrs. Sunday. She was a very old woman who lived in a decaying house on the hill.

The kids in the neighborhood liked to believe that Mrs. Sunday was a vampire and that her house

was "haunted." On warm days the two friends imagined they saw Mrs. Sunday, old and ghostlike, sitting on her broken-down porch. But they never dared to get close enough to *really* see her.

Sometimes, when Tino and Samuel went snooping in her yard, Mrs. Sunday would come to her door and cry, in a determined voice, "What do you children want? What are you doing in my yard?" This was always the highlight of their daily adventures. They would dash back to the street, shouting and pretending to be more terrified than they were.

"Boy," Samuel would say, "that was a close one! She almost got us."

One day after school, Tino and Samuel were passing Mrs. Sunday's house. They had no plans to snoop that day because it was Wednesday, the day they had to get to Little League. Suddenly they heard a voice call, "Oh, boys! Would you come here, please? I need your help." Tino did not have time to understand the words fully before he saw Samuel take off at a gallop down the hill, shouting, "It's the ghost. Let's get out of here!"

"Young man, would you help me, please?" Tino heard the voice say again. He was about to turn and dash down the hill with Samuel, but something seemed to hold him and make him stay.

"My screen door is stuck," she said. "I can't get it open. Would you see if you can do it for me?"

Tino was not certain what he should do. He felt drawn to the voice. He entered the yard. There he saw Mrs. Sunday for the first time. She was very old and dressed all in black. She looked like the witches he had seen at Halloween time.

Cautiously Tino walked onto the porch.

"Don't be afraid," she said. "I won't eat you."

Tino went right to work. He took a firm grip on the handle of the screen door, fixed his feet solidly on the rotting boards of the porch, and pulled with all his might. Amazingly, the screen door came completely off its rusted hinges and fell across Tino, pinning him to the floor.

It had happened, he thought—he had fallen into her trap. She would have him in her power. Though he wasn't hurt and felt no pain, he was frightened and stunned.

After a moment, he saw fuzzily through the torn screen that Mrs. Sunday was laughing uncontrollably, her tiny body rocking with merriment.

"Forgive me," she said, laughing. "I can't help it. You look so funny. I won't ever have to worry about the door sticking again, will I?"

Tino wriggled out from under the screen, more embarrassed than harmed.

"Are you all right?" Mrs. Sunday said.

"Yeah," Tino replied, his heart pounding hard under his T-shirt.

"Now that the door is gone," Mrs. Sunday continued, chuckling, "it will be easier to go in and out of the house. So why don't you come on in and I'll get you a treat for your trouble."

"No, thanks," Tino was quick to respond. He remembered his parents' warnings about taking food from strangers. "I've got to get to Little League."

"Well," Mrs. Sunday said, "then why don't you stop by tomorrow on your way home from school? I'll have something special for you."

"No, thanks," Tino muttered, eager to get away. "It's okay."

"I want to give you a reward for helping me. Come by after school. You don't have to stay if you don't want to."

"Well . . ." Tino hesitated.

"Will you come? I don't want to make a surprise for nothing."

"Okay."

"By the way, what's your name?" Mrs. Sunday asked.

"Tino," he replied.

"That's a nice name. Mine's Gladys Sunday. Now if you'll just lean the door against the wall, you can get along to your baseball game."

Tino did what she asked. There was something about the sound of Mrs. Sunday's voice that made him feel good. He especially liked the way she said his name. She made it sound as if it belonged to him alone, in all the world.

"Good-bye, Tino," she said. "See you tomorrow."

"Good-bye," Tino responded, and dashed off to his game.

CHAPTER TWO

THE FRIENDSHIP

Tino did not tell Samuel about his visit with Mrs. Sunday. There was something about that meeting he wanted to keep secret. He did ask his mother if he could visit Mrs. Sunday again. He told her about the adventure with the screen door and his promise to return.

"Do you think it's okay?" he asked.

"She's the woman who lives on the hill? Of course you may visit her. I've heard she's a very nice person. But if you do go, don't forget your manners."

Even though he was still a little hesitant, as soon as school was out the next day Tino returned to Mrs. Sunday's house. She was sitting on her porch. Tino noticed the softness in her eyes and the warmth she showed in her smile.

"Tino," Mrs. Sunday called to him. "You've come. I was hoping you would. I have your surprise. Cookies. Just baked this morning." She pointed to a plate on the table, piled high with cookies. "Those are for you. Why don't you sit down and eat a few? You can take the others home with you for your mother and father." She pointed to a chair at her side.

"Thank you," he said, remembering his manners.

For a moment, he wondered if the cookies might have some magical potion that would put him to sleep, or worse yet, kill him, but he dismissed the idea. His mother said that Mrs. Sunday was kind, and he could see that she was. He sat down and bit into a cookie. It was delicious, just like the cookies his grandmother Lelia made when he visited her each summer.

"Good?" Mrs. Sunday smiled.

"Uh huh," Tino responded.

"I used to make them for my children," she said.

Tino ate a second cookie while Mrs. Sunday watched. He wondered what to say next to someone so old, but he didn't have to worry about it.

"Do you live close by, Tino?" Mrs. Sunday continued the conversation.

"In the brown house down the hill, by the corner. On Fairmount."

"Oh yes. I know it. The Thomases used to live there a long time ago."

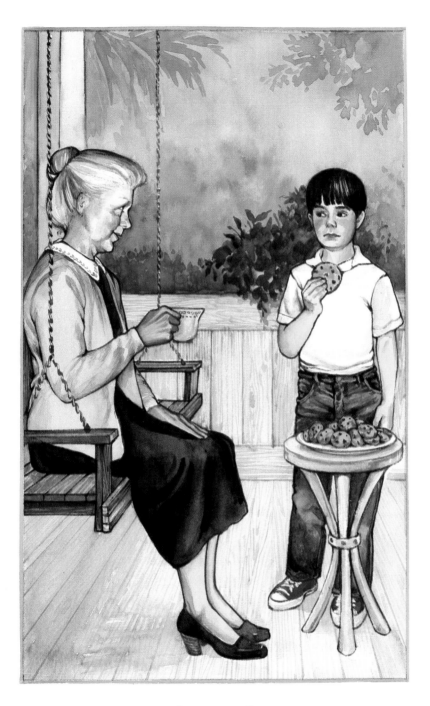

"I live there now with my mom and dad."

"And brothers and sisters?"

"Un uh, just me."

"Dear me, an only child. Being an only child can sometimes be very lonely. In my day," Mrs. Sunday said, "we had big families. I had eight children."

"Eight! Wow!" Tino said, stuffing another cookie into his mouth. The idea that they might have some magic potion seemed silly to him by this time.

"Do they live here, too?" Tino asked.

"No. My heavens, no. Not anymore. They did

once, a long time ago. They're all gone now." After a moment, she added, "I live here by myself."

"Don't they come and visit you?" Tino asked, puzzled.

"They used to, but they're far away, and it's not easy for them to visit. They call me and they write to me when they think about it. You know, holidays and birthdays."

"Why don't you go live with them?" Tino asked.

"They want me to, and I might someday. But I've been in this house for a very long time. It's full of memories. It's hard to part with the past. Do you know what I mean?" Then she laughed. "But of course not. Children are too busy living *now* to collect memories. It's nice to have someone to talk with. I miss having people around." She paused thoughtfully for a moment, then she brightened. "I have a wonderful idea," she said, with excitement in her voice. "Maybe you'd like to be my friend?"

"I don't know," Tino answered awkwardly. He didn't know what he'd do with such an *old* friend. "I'm pretty busy."

"It won't take a lot to be my friend," she said. "You can just stop by when you feel like it. We'll talk and eat cookies and pass the time together. Maybe we can make new memories. One is never too young or old to make memories. Lasting memories of happiness can someday make all the difference."

"Well," Tino stammered, "I guess I can come by once in a while. I'll ask my mom."

Mrs. Sunday extended her small, thin hand. "I hope it will be all right," she said, smiling. Tino took her hand and held it briefly. It was surprisingly warm.

CHAPTER THREE

THE DECISION

Tino shared Mrs. Sunday's cookies with his parents at dinner that night.

"These are delicious cookies," his father exclaimed. "Who made them?"

"Mrs. Sunday, the woman who lives up on the hill."

"Oh," his father said, "the one who has that run-down house?"

"Yeah, but it's not her fault that it's run-down," Tino said. "She doesn't have anyone to fix it for her."

"Then she shouldn't live there," his father said. "There are homes for older people, places where they can be taken care of."

"But she can't leave her memories," Tino said.
"Memories?" his mother questioned.
"Mrs. Sunday told me all about her memories."
When dinner was over, Tino and his father went outside and played catch. It felt good. Later, just before he fell asleep, Tino's mother came into his room, as she always did, to say good night. Tino

asked, "What can you do to make someone feel unlonesome?"

"Well," his mother answered, busily tucking the blankets around him, "you let them know you care about them. You spend time with them. You give them things that make them happy. But most of all, you love them."

"Are you lonely, Mom?" Tino asked.

His mother seemed surprised that he would ask such a question. She hesitated for a moment. "I guess everyone is lonely at times. But I'm lucky. I have your father and friends and you."

"Do you have memories, too?"

"Oh yes, lots of them."

"Mom," he asked, "is it all right if I make Mrs. Sunday my friend? I think she's real lonesome."

"Of course." His mother smiled as she kissed him good night. "I'm sure she'll make a great friend."

Tino fell asleep wondering what it was like to have a memory.

The following morning, Mrs. Sunday was still on Tino's mind. He felt that he wanted to do something to help her be "unlonely." She had suggested that they be friends. He wondered what they could do when they were together. They couldn't throw stones at the date palms or annoy the Wilsons' dog or play baseball or go for hikes. They could only sit and talk. And what would they find to talk about?

Still, Tino knew that he had to do something. For starters, he thought he could tell her about the model cars he made. In fact, he could bring one for her to see. "Anyway," he made up his mind, "I'm going to be her friend."

CHAPTER FOUR

THE SHARING

Tino brought his favorite miniature car, the Packard, to school the next day. It was the car that had taken him and his father the longest time to make, and it was his favorite. He wrapped it carefully in a handkerchief and packed it into his lunch box.

Mrs. Sunday was on her porch when Tino arrived.

"Tino, what a nice surprise." Mrs. Sunday seemed very happy to see him. It made him feel good. "My first visitor today," she said.

"I brought something to show you," he said. "It's a model of an old car they don't make anymore. It was called a Packard." He held it out to her. She took it carefully into her hands.

"You made this?" she asked. "It's beautiful! You know, a long time ago we had a real Packard."

"You had a *real* Packard?"

"I know I have pictures of it somewhere. Wouldn't it be fun to find them? Come and look," Mrs. Sunday said. Tino followed her into the living room. It was very dark inside. Still, he was surprised to see how nice it was. Everything was very old: framed photographs, paintings, vases, glasses, books, and old-fashioned lamps everywhere.

"Let's see," said Mrs. Sunday, "I think the photo albums are in that large cupboard over there, under those boxes. You can get to them more easily than I can." Tino rummaged among the boxes where Mrs. Sunday pointed.

"That's it . . . there," she said. Tino carefully took out the large photo album.

"Oh dear. Look at the dust. It's been a long time since I've looked at this. Now, let's see. There's more light by the window. We can raise the shade."

Tino raised the shade. Warm sunlight streamed into the room and swallowed the darkness.

Mrs. Sunday said, "It's much nicer with the shades raised. I can't imagine why I've been living in the dark."

They settled side by side, and Mrs. Sunday opened the album.

"Here I am with my husband, Ben, when we were first married. Can you imagine that I ever looked so young?"

She showed him another photograph. "And these are my children."

Quickly she turned a few more pages. "Ah, here it is!" she said, touching a photo of a shiny, black automobile. "Just look at that! Isn't it beautiful? Riding in that car always made me feel so good. We'd pile the children in on Sundays and have such a good time. I loved that Packard," she said, "and

now my new friend Tino has a Packard and it's *his* favorite, too."

They both laughed. "These photographs are full of memories for me," Mrs. Sunday told Tino. "Every picture tells its own story. My past is on every page." Tino wondered why she had tears in her eyes if her memories were as nice as she said they were.

Afterward they sat at the kitchen table and drank milk and ate fresh gingersnaps. Tino liked being

with Mrs. Sunday. She was not like other grown-ups. She spoke right to him and listened to him as if he were really there. Most of all, she was interested in him and in the things he was doing.

"You know," Tino stammered, rather ashamed, "before I knew you, I was afraid of you."

"Afraid of me?" Mrs. Sunday laughed. "Oh, Tino, you can see that there is so little of me to be afraid of." After a moment, she asked, "And what do you think now?"

"I think you're real nice," Tino said, matter-of-factly. "And you smell good."

CHAPTER FIVE

THE GIFT

Tino's visits with Mrs. Sunday were happening more and more often. She always seemed happy to see him, no matter how often he came.

He especially liked to hear about her memories. She told him about growing up, about sad and happy times with her family, about the olden days when her house was beautiful and the only one on the hill, about when the city had streetcars, before television sets, about when her children went away and her husband died. It always made him sad when he had to leave Mrs. Sunday alone.

Once Tino asked Mrs. Sunday what she did when he wasn't there. "Well, not much that's exciting," she said.

"Don't you watch TV?" was Tino's next question.

"I know you won't believe it, but I haven't got one. In fact, I haven't had one since my old black-and-white set stopped working years ago."

It suddenly occurred to Tino that a TV set might help Mrs. Sunday to be less lonely. But where would he get a TV set to give her? That night, when he was watching one of his favorite programs, the idea came to him. Of course. It was simple. He'd give Mrs. Sunday the family television set. They didn't need it as much as she did.

The next day Tino told Samuel about his plan.

"That doesn't sound like such a good idea to me. Your mom and dad will kill you," Samuel said.

"They almost never watch TV. I don't think they'll even know it's gone."

"But what about you? You'll miss all the good shows."

"I know, but there are other things I can do. Will you help me bring it to Mrs. Sunday's house?"

"Not me," said Samuel. "I'm not going to get in trouble with your mom and dad."

"They won't care," Tino assured him.

"Well, okay," Samuel finally agreed, "but I wouldn't want to be you when they see it's gone."

Even with Samuel's help it wasn't easy to get the television set to Mrs. Sunday's house. She was astonished when she saw the two boys struggling up the path, with the television set dangerously balanced on a wagon.

"What's this?" she asked.

"It's a TV," Tino said. "I brought it for you, for when you're alone."

"But where did you get it?" Mrs. Sunday questioned.

"Well, it's ours," Tino answered, "but we're not using it."

"A television set!" Mrs. Sunday exclaimed, delighted. "I haven't had a television set for years."

"Now you can watch baseball games and soap operas and quiz shows and all kinds of things," Tino said excitedly.

He could see that Mrs. Sunday was very pleased. It made him feel good to be giving his friend such a splendid gift. It felt even better than when someone gave him something.

CHAPTER SIX

THE DISAGREEMENT

Tino's father came home about six-thirty that evening. As usual, he greeted everyone with a hug and disappeared into his bedroom to change his clothes. In a few minutes, he was back in the kitchen offering to help. Tino's mother asked his father to make the salad. Tino, in the meantime, set the table. It was nice to do things together.

Tino forgot about the TV set until after dinner, when his father asked, "Anything good on TV tonight?" Tino's heart stopped for a moment. Here it comes, he thought. By this time his father was in the living room. "Hey," Tino heard him call, "what's happened to the television set?"

Tino was silent.

"Where's the TV?" his father repeated.

"What do you mean?" Tino's mother asked, getting up from the table.

"It's gone. The TV's gone," his father said. Tino's mother walked into the living room.

"Are you having it fixed?" his father continued, puzzled.

Then Tino heard his mother's voice. "It *is* gone! How could it be? It was here this morning. There isn't anything else missing, is there?"

"It doesn't seem so," his father answered.

Tino knew he had waited long enough, but he couldn't think of what to say. Finally he spoke. "I gave it away," he said simply.

"You what?" his parents said at the same time, coming back into the kitchen.

"I gave it away."

"You gave it away!?"

"Yeah."

"You gave away the family television set?" his father asked in disbelief. "Are you crazy? Who did you give it to?"

"To Mrs. Sunday."

"Who?" Tino could tell that his father's patience was running out.

"My friend who lives on the hill."

"The friend who lives on the hill?" his father repeated, with growing frustration.

"The lady I was telling you about."

"Lady? What lady?"

"The one I told you about."

"I don't remember any lady you told me about!" his father exclaimed with mounting anger.

"Now, calm down," Tino's mother said. "I think I know who he's talking about." She reached out to Tino and lifted his lowered head. "You mean the lonely woman?"

"Yeah, Mrs. Sunday, the lady who's all alone," Tino explained, holding back his tears.

"You *gave* her our television set?" his mother asked.

"She needs it," Tino said. "I didn't think you

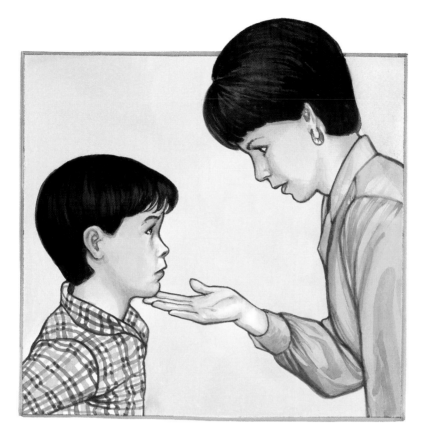

cared about TV anyway. You always say you don't."

"Well, that's not the point," his father said angrily. "You can't just decide to give away the family TV without asking."

"Mom said that if we wanted to make people unlonely, we should give them things...." Tears began to well up into his eyes. He knew he wouldn't be able to defend himself further. They just wouldn't understand.

"That may be true," his father said, "but a TV isn't

a small thing. You know you should have asked."

By this time, Tino was crying in quiet frustration. "But she's so old," he sobbed, "and she's all alone. And she has no friends. And a TV would keep her company."

"But what about us?" his father continued.

"We don't need a TV set as much as she does. We've got lots of other things."

Tino's mother took him into her arms and held him close. "It's okay, Tino," she said. "You meant to do a good thing. It's just that we're upset that you didn't think to ask us."

Tino said, finally defeated, "I'm sorry."

"Why don't you go up to your room? We all need to calm down before we decide what to do about this," his mother said. Tino left the room, wiping his tears with the back of his hand.

"So now what?" his mother said to Tino's father.

"We'll just have to go and get it back. Wouldn't you think that an old lady like that would know better than to take such an expensive gift from a child?" his father grumbled.

"But you know," Tino's mother said thoughtfully, "it was a very nice thing for Tino to do."

"A nice thing!" his father exclaimed.

"Yes."

"What do you mean?"

"Think about it. He wanted to make her happy.

He did it in the best way he knew how. Of course, he should have asked, but what he did was really thoughtful. And we're showing him by our anger that it was wrong."

After a moment, Tino's father answered, "Yes, I guess you're right."

"Why don't you go up and talk with him?"

"What can I say?"

"You'll think of something."

"And what about the TV?"

"Why don't you ask Tino and see what he suggests?"

Tino's father went upstairs. Sitting down on the bed next to Tino, he said, "I'm sorry I got so upset. I know that you just wanted to help Mrs. Sunday, and that was good. But you can't just give away our things without asking."

"Yeah, I know," Tino said softly. "She's a nice lady, Dad. I like her a lot." After a few seconds, he added, "I'll go get the TV back."

"No," his father said. "Not now. Let's wait until tomorrow."

Tino leaned closer to his father. He felt better now.

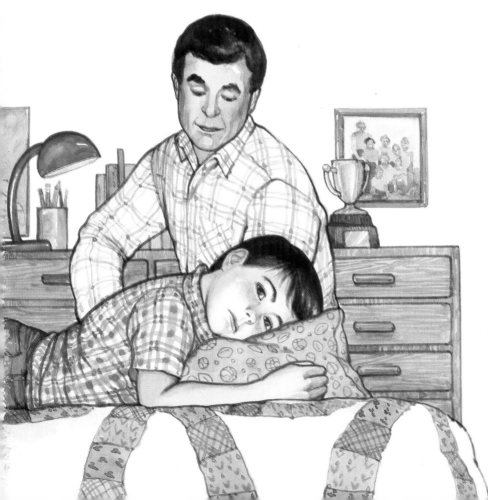

CHAPTER SEVEN

A MEMORY FOR TINO

The next day was Saturday. Tino decided that it would be best to go to Mrs. Sunday's house early to explain what happened. When he arrived at her house, she greeted him in her happy, warm way. It was difficult for Tino to look at her. She seemed to notice instantly that something was wrong.

"Tino, what's the matter?" Mrs. Sunday stopped what she was doing and wiped her hands on her apron. He didn't answer. "I watched TV last night," she said, trying to cheer him up. "I saw a wonderful show about wild animals. You were right, Tino, it was good company for me. I love your present."

Now, Tino thought, it was going to be even harder to tell her the news that she was going to have to give it back.

After a moment, she asked again, "Is there something the matter? Whatever is bothering you, Tino, you can tell me." She sat on a chair beside him. "Remember, we're friends."

"Well," Tino stammered, "my mom and dad found out about the TV set. They're real mad."

"I don't understand," said Mrs. Sunday. "I thought no one was using the television."

"I didn't ask them if I could take it. I didn't think they'd care."

"Oh, Tino," Mrs. Sunday said. "I'm sorry. Well, no harm done. We'll just have to find a way to give it back. I'll write a note to your father and mother explaining what happened. I'm sure they'll understand."

When he went home, Tino put the note Mrs. Sunday had written on the kitchen table where his mother would find it, and went to his room.

"Where's Tino?" his father said.

"I think I heard him come in just a little while ago," said Tino's mother. "He could be in his room."

"Well, we'd better call him. It's time to pay Mrs. Sunday a visit."

"Before we do that, I think you should read this note. Tino must have left it on the table when he came in. He's already been to Mrs. Sunday's. He's already told her."

Tino's father read the note:

My dear friends,

I am so sorry about what happened. I'm afraid that I did not understand that Tino had given me the family television set. Of course it will be returned at once. It's not important.

What is important is the gift of friendship that Tino has given me. At this point in my life, it is among my most prized possessions. Tino is a very special child. You must be very proud to have raised such a fine boy.

Please come to visit sometime. It would bring me great joy to meet you and to offer my apology personally.

Cordially,
Gladys Sunday

"It makes me feel a little ashamed," Tino's mother said. "Tino is just a child, and yet he's wiser than we are."

"You mean you think we should let her keep the set?" Tino's father asked.

"Why not? Who cares about it anyway? Maybe if we gave it away, we'd find more time to be together as a family."

"Maybe you're right," he said.

When Tino came into the kitchen, his father said,

"We need to talk to you." He sat down with his parents. He was sure that they would scold him again for what he had done.

"We've been thinking a lot about Mrs. Sunday," his father told him. "We think we've been wrong about the TV set, especially about getting so upset."

"You mean she can keep the set?" Tino said, surprised.

"Yes."

"Gee, that's great. When can we tell her?"

"As soon as you think she'd be ready," answered his mother.

"Now?" Tino asked.

"If you think so."

"Sure!"

"But should we drop in without telling her we're coming?" his mother wondered.

"Oh sure, she never goes anywhere. I know it would be all right."

It didn't take them much time to get up the hill.

Tino knocked on the front door. Mrs. Sunday looked very surprised when she saw her visitors.

"This is my mom and dad," Tino said. "They wanted to come and see you. I told them it would be okay."

"I hope it is," Tino's mother said.

"Oh yes, of course. Come in," Mrs. Sunday said, and led them into her living room. "I'm so glad you've come. I've been wanting to meet you. I'm sorry about the misunderstanding. The television set is over there. You can take it anytime."

Tino's mother said quickly, "Oh no. We want you to keep the set."

"Oh, I couldn't do that," Mrs. Sunday said.

"Yes," Tino's father interrupted, "please."

Mrs. Sunday protested, "I couldn't!"

Tino's mother pleaded. "You would do us all a big favor."

"I don't know what to say," Mrs. Sunday said softly. "It's so very nice of you."

Tino felt such happiness, and he could tell that his dad and mom did, too.

Mrs. Sunday said, "Tino and I planned a picnic in the backyard this afternoon. Maybe you'd like to join us?"

Tino's parents exchanged a quick approving glance.

"Yes, we'd love to stay if you let us help."

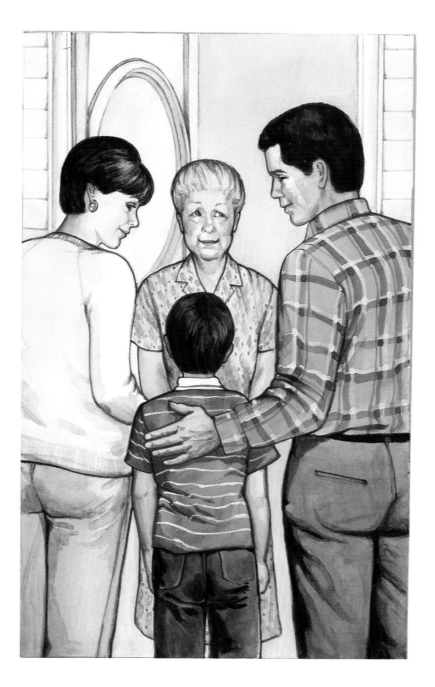

Tino's mother went into the kitchen with Mrs. Sunday. They chatted excitedly about what they might prepare for the picnic. Tino said to his father, "Dad, I'm sorry about the TV."

His father smiled and scooped Tino into his arms. "I'm not!" he said and carried him out into the yard.

When everyone was settled around the picnic blanket, Mrs. Sunday reached out and took Tino's

hand. "None of this would have happened, Tino,"
she said, "if it hadn't been for you."

Tino wanted to say something, but he could not
find the words. He knew he would never forget this
moment. He had given something to Mrs. Sunday,
something that might break or be lost. But she had
given him something better—more lasting—a
memory of happiness. And he had never had such
a special memory until now.

AFTERWORD

To my friend the reader,

Too often we have an experience and immediately after it's over we let it go. Then it is lost to us forever. Experiences, as well as memories, can be captured and kept only when we take the time to think about them. Many of us live only for today. We fail to realize that it is our memories that give life its meaning and structure. We must keep them alive.

For this reason, after reading *A Memory for Tino*, it might be fun to talk about it with people you love. The following questions may help you to start:

What does it mean to have a memory? Are memories always happy? Can a sad memory be a good memory? What are some of your happy memories? What are some of your sad memories?

What does it mean to be lonely? Have you ever been lonely? Why was Mrs. Sunday lonely? Does how old you are have anything to do with loneliness? Can anyone, at any age, be lonely?

Was giving the family television set to Mrs. Sunday a good thing for Tino to do? Did Samuel miss something by not becoming Mrs. Sunday's friend? Why did giving make Tino so happy?

LEO BUSCAGLIA has been an educator for over thirty years. He spent much of his early career teaching in the elementary schools, giving him a special understanding of children. Currently, Dr. Buscaglia is a professor of education at the University of Southern California.

An enormously popular lecturer who attracts standing-room-only audiences throughout the country, Dr. Buscaglia's appearances on public and network television have made him a friend to millions. His previous books include *Loving Each Other*; *Living, Loving, and Learning*; *Bus Nine to Paradise*; *Seven Stories of Christmas Love*; and *The Fall of Freddie the Leaf*.

Quality Printing By:
United Lithographing Corporation
47-47 32nd Place
Long Island City, NY 11101 U.S.A.